PENGUIN BOOK

ITS DAY BEING GONE

ROSE MCLARNEY is the author of *The Always Broken Plates of Mountains*. She has been awarded the Fellowship of Southern Writers' biennial George Garrett New Writing Award for Poetry, Alligator Juniper's 2011 National Poetry Prize, and the Joan Beebe Fellowship at Warren Wilson College. Her poems have appeared in *The Kenyon Review, Orion, Slate, New England Review,* and many other journals. A graduate of Warren Wilson's MFA Program for Writers, she currently teaches poetry at Oklahoma State University.

THE NATIONAL POETRY SERIES

The National Poetry Series was established in 1978 to ensure the publication of five poetry books annually through five participating publishers. Publication is funded each year by the Lannan Foundation, Stephen Graham, Juliet Lea Hillman Simonds, and The Poetry Foundation. For a complete listing of generous contributors to the National Poetry Series, please visit www.nationalpoetryseries.org.

2013 COMPETITION WINNERS

Ampersand Revisited
by Simeon Berry of Somerville, Massachusetts
Chosen by Ariana Reines, to be published by Fence Books

Trespass
by Thomas Dooley of New York, New York
Chosen by Charlie Smith,
to be published by HarperCollins Publishers

Bone Map
by Sara Eliza Johnson of Salt Lake City, Utah
Chosen by Martha Collins, to be published by Milkweed Editions

Its Day Being Gone
by Rose McLarney of Tulsa, Oklahoma
Chosen by Robert Wrigley, to be published by Penguin Books

What Ridiculous Things We Could Ask of Each Other
by Jeffrey Schultz of Los Angeles, California
Chosen by Kevin Young, to be published by University of Georgia Press

ITS DAY BEING GONE

ROSE MCLARNEY

PENGUIN BOOKS

PENGUIN BOOKS
Published by the Penguin Group
Penguin Group (USA) LLC
375 Hudson Street
New York, New York 10014

USA | Canada | UK | Ireland | Australia | New Zealand | India | South Africa | China

penguin.com
A Penguin Random House Company

First published in Penguin Books 2014

Pages vii–viii constitute an extension of this copyright page.
McLarney, Rose, 1982–
Its day being gone / Rose McLarney.
pages cm. — (National Poetry Series)
ISBN 978-0-14-312657-7 (paperback)
I. Title.
PS3613.C5725A2 2014
811'.6—dc23
2014006355

Printed in the United States of America

1   3   5   7   9   10   8   6   4   2

Set in Spectrum MT Std
Designed by Ginger Legato

For J.

(May my stories, hereafter, also be yours.)

ACKNOWLEDGMENTS

Sincere thanks to the editors of publications in which the following poems first appeared, some in slightly different forms and under different titles:

"Redemption," "Watershed," "Arcadia," "How History Would Have It": *Missouri Review.*

"Guts, Gleam": *Valparaiso Poetry Review.*

"Electrification": *Orion.*

"Past Lives": *The Freeman.*

"Imminent Domain," "And Inside Winged Beings Sleep," "To Tell Us Why We're Here," "Exotica," "Tribute," "Love Poem," "Into Another," "The Language for This," "Aloof Above," "In Proportion," "Light Colored," "The Same as Anyone," "Setting," "Reprise," "Tributaries of the Same Body": *Hone Creek*, an online chapbook from *Mudlark.*

"Landscape": *Cimarron Review.*

"Wet Not with Weeping": *Missouri Review.*

"Story with a Real Beast and a Little Blood in It": *Slate.*

"Petition": *The Greensboro Review.*

"To Boys with Names Like Wiley, or Loyal": *Mead: The Magazine of Literature and Libations.*

"Eyes Lifted": *Southern Humanities Review*

"Facing North," "The Model Walks Away from a Job," "I Float," What Music Should Accompany This": *Waxwing*

"Home Fires": *Still: The Journal*

"Native Species": *Construction*

"What the Snake Says," "My Gift," "How to See," " The Treatment Was Frogs, or, The Tradition Was Honey," "Conservators," Glossing the Image": *Comnotations Press*

CONTENTS

I. FOLK TALE

2. ANOTHER WORLD

3. ANOTHER TELLING

Little Margaret, sitting at her high hall door,
Combing back her long, yellow hair,
When she saw Sweet William and his new-made bride
Riding from the church so near.

Down she throwed her ivory comb,
Back she throwed her hair,
Saying, "I'll go down and bid him farewell,
And nevermore go there."

Its day being gone and night coming on,
When most all men were asleep,
Little Margaret appeared all dressed in white,
A-standing at their bed-feet.

—from "Little Margaret," an Appalachian ballad

ITS DAY BEING GONE

▪ 1 ▪

FOLKTALE

How articulate, the eyes
of silent animals when I chose
to shoot the sick goat. All day,
the dogs would not look at me, not
let me touch them, legs folding away from
the level to which I had lowered my hand.

And the chickens ran,
following their crazed paths,
every which way, but every way
away from me. The goat
looked as if she were running
as she lay, after, legs kicking.

But don't chickens always run
like that? And this is no new
remorse. The light has always
been leaving my narrow,
north section. Place of the long
history of short days.

It's the frost that stays. More mornings
than not here, no sun is enough
to undo the frost. I should have given
her southerly pasture. I should have
gone in another direction.

But consider where goats live
the world over. They browse
on woody brush. On rock, on cliffs.
In deserts, harsh habitat. They choose
cursed land. Who chooses goats?

I chose goats. I liked the bone shapes
in their eyes, the strange, slit pupils
they turned to me, chewing the corners
of my heavy coat. I wanted to live here,
on an old hardscrabble farm.

In this era, when there is no need
to farm, who is drawn to have livestock,
which die so much? Piss and blood
pour out of the back of a shot body.
But it's piss and blood keeping them
alive too. Cleaning the stalls, cleaning
the wounds common to animals so curious.

She worked herself through fences,
under walls. She worked her head into my
pockets. Worked her way in
to every opening.

What's different about a dead body
is what comes from the other end,
a great cursive scrawl of steam
from the mouth. It is the last word,
soundless, without the stop and start
of syllables, definitive.

What comes from the mouth
blows away. Didn't I say
I was done with livestock last winter
when the calf froze to the ground, then to
death because it couldn't move?

When I ripped it loose, the intestines,
threaded through crow-torn holes
in its belly, clung to the grass and shattered.

I said those were my ties to the place.
They were too cold to bleed. A quick job
to clean up and bury, I claimed.

I said I would never use animals
as the figures for my sorrows again.
But when the goat dropped shot,
the bread I'd brought to get her
to put her head down still in her teeth,
the chickens pecked at it.

I'm still here. I can't stay away
from the hard images. Bread
taken from her mouth even then.

Is it neglect that knots
the fruit of old apple and pear trees,
studs sweetness with hard spots?
Or are the people who planted them,
stabbed them with grafts, still working
branches, warping them with windy hands,
so we'll know how it is to age?

And is the barn suffering from disuse,
or was it a cane or shoe heels tapping
the rooftop, some couple lying
in their grave, their dream of dancing,
that poked through tin, so we'd have to
patch it? So I'd have to stand inside
staring at the spot of sun while my love
worked up there with a bucket of tar,
watching as the brilliant was
blacked out?

Yes, much of what you grew up with had already faded—
there was less paint than rust on the metal, and littler
hope. Excepting memory and the hydrangea—

those were strange bright because your women
were just enough short of weary to pour ashes
around flowers and turn them blue. About memory—

looking back is the one thing you're true to, that circling
the one ring you'll wear, like the ring run
through the nose of a bull. That's sharp enough—

the pull on the tenderest part, to move even a beast.

The dark didn't scare her.
It's this way days

have grown long, like distances
between them of an evening.

It used to be they gathered
at the fire, had to draw near.

Maybe her husband played music,
but there was nothing more

to do until dawn. Since he's been
working at the sawmill, and cut

the stand of wild cherry, she can see
town glowing in the valley, hear

the saws sing, but not him.
He doesn't come home

until the coals are cold.
She eats in the kitchen while she cooks,

and reads the news, leaning into
the stove hood for its light.

The boy wants to get to town too.
Quick, eats what she hands him,

standing under the porch bulb,
while moths fly against it

and drop singed around them.
Then her son steps out

into the night.

These are the ghosts that gather at dawn,
drawn to light and company: the men
who meet each day at the auto shop counter
to talk of work, of what can be kept working.

The mechanic's second job
may be grading, cutting building sites
into the mountain where he grew up,
but he says his memories of being a child
in those woods are *vivid*, pronouncing the *i*
so it stretches long into a *y,* goes deep,
and buries itself in the earth again.

The truck driver (that's what he does for money)
is truly a farrier and tells of the lame horse
he has come from treating. Just touching
the tendons of her legs, he could tell
she had a strain from standing in mud.
Of course, they feel the shifting ground.

On the hardest of mornings
in winter, they watch each other appear
through frosted windows, smoking
and so doubly clouded.
Lifting hands to mouths, they could be
blowing good-bye kisses.

Before bed, I read folktales about ghost cats
that rolled in fire, spoke though headless,
and ran newcomers from old houses.
But my dreams were welcome ones,
of the school playground where we
scratched specks of garnet out of the dirt.
That's the last place I saw my friend, until today,
visiting home, taking a back route behind
the shopping plaza. On break in an apron,
there was a woman who had to be her—
that was a face I grew up with—turning out
cans of food by the dumpster. Cats
coursed from the abandoned orchard, arcing
their backs toward her hand, with a cigarette
burning in it.

I walked the dirt road
every morning that summer,
up switchbacks, weaving
like a tracked rabbit.

A few houses on bits of flat
kept their backs to the walls
of mountains, knowing
their place, beneath the peaks,

for the first mile. Then, higher,
there was pure forest,
nothing fouling it, no buildings,

and no traffic either. Except
one man pulling a bulldozer
to work, who often paused
to roll down the window

and whisper his warning,
Careful out here alone.
Big cat will get you.

Puma, panther, painter,
ghost cat, shadow cat,
cougar, catamount,
mountain screamer—

all my life, I've been hearing
people speak the names
of the mountain lion.

But few ever see one.
Maybe they talk of the animal
to cause each other fright,

maybe for a kind of comfort,
keeping alive the belief
that what wildness abides
out there is the danger.

That summer, I trusted the cat
would stop, not cross
the tree line. What I listened for were
tires, cutting back in my direction.

Even if the man never did
turn toward me, take hold,
I would have been right to fear him.
In time, I saw his way. Forcing

new roads through trees
was his work. He was there to bare
where they'd given cover,

and no lion ever would
walk there again, no girl.

In the swayback structures
of the downtown deserted when the new
road turned away from it, there is still
a reason to visit, some business.

There's a sport shop, run by
a blind man. He listens to you walk
and can tell where you are: in arrows,
an aisle down from sights,
with the releases behind you,
scent blocker in plain view.

Bring him your bow, and he'll know
the make and model within minutes,
running his fingers over the limb,
strumming the string slowly.

You'll have to move on, eventually,
driving through what might have been
familiar features, the rises and lows
of the land. But you won't recognize
anything for sure anymore, since
the place has become
a bypass, strip.

It's just as well he can't see and stays
in the dark of the shop, remembering
when his arms were tight with muscle,
trees crowded together, trunks close,
and deer coursed thick between.

Go see him, holding his old bow
in the store just outside the sprawl.
The blind man imagines
that it can, even now,
be drawn all the way back.

A skinned bear looks like a human. A shot bear
always falls on his back, like he's looking
at heaven. Human bodies are also like another's—
made in his image, it is said, by those who can believe
that after this world we will go on to another.
Making symbols, comparing one thing to the next,
then another, in all this familiar, comforting likening
I can forget where I began. That skinned body,
limbs spread for cutting, can I say now it looks like
it is ready for an angel's flight?
                            But if we want allegory,
                            what of this conclusion?

When bears grow old and their teeth wear down
too far to tear, they come out of deep woods
into orchards to feed on apples, reaching up
for soft fruit with heavy paws. They stand
like humans. Are bears like humans, haunted
by deaths or the less definite and so ceaseless losses
that are love? Do bears too imagine understanding
that comes at the end, hope for redemption?
Now, in the orchards, in the open—this is the time
when it is easiest to see the bears, to get them
in the rifle's sights.

The bawl of a hound trailing an animal
rises when he crosses a ridgetop,
rushes when he fords a creek. His howl,
heard down in the bottom, is a single sense's map
of the land beyond here, and I listen.
I stay where mountains cut off any view, and I listen.
I lie in the laurel hells, bushes covering slopes
so thickly not even the sun can crawl through,
where listen is all I can do. I listen wanting to be
a blind believer. But it's not in me, the purity
of feeling of a dog with a rabbit between his teeth,
in the moment when he turns to run toward
his master.

I tried to leave behind
everything that could make me
burn, to evade the urges
of change, by shutting myself up

in the country. I live apart,
I stay in and spend evenings
on quiet pursuits, studying
history. What I've learned

is that the old house I chose
for its worn, creaking wood
was built after a woman
torched her first home,

that desperate for something
new. It's to the house of her
wanting, her flame azaleas
all around, growing in closer,

where I have come to simplify
my desires. I wade in the creek,
collecting from the water pieces
of china, edges charred.

It was nearly still water, that river,
with no rapids talking, but she learned from it
the fish. First, noticing the one with a hard
maw for scraping the algae she ate off stone,
then all the ways beings were made to live
in those parts.

Molly crawl bottom had a downturned mouth
for bottom feeding. The commonest
fish, living even in ditches, Mollies found ways
to make do. And she could identify them
in however much murk because of how long
she'd spent staring at the same places.

The lamprey eel had a sucker face.
Seven years, she stayed burrowed in the mud,
blind. Then, in one week, she emerged, grew eyes,
bit on to a rock, and waited to mate. Males
let sperm drift and she loosed her eggs.
That was her peak, her purpose, and she died.
That's what became of her when she went out
looking—a lesson as easy to identify
as the long lines of the eel among any other species.

Sunfish had little upturned lips for pecking
insects from the surface, and were broad like sails,
because they were from slow corners.
The way their flattened forms were swept
downstream by the slightest current looked like
an argument for staying where you belong.
For moving like the wives who hugged
corners when they passed through rooms, slipped

into kitchens where dishwater made their voices
unknowns beneath its gushing.

Mouths can say enough about the way you are
without making a sound. That's the sort of thing
she'd been taught to—tried to, for years—tell herself
when she watched the river and saw that water
ran away.

So inelegant, your arms and legs,
that wrapped around the one you loved.
It seems they still pretend to.

At least, it doesn't look like limbs help much,
seeing you scrabble up proud mountains, thrash
through old brush.

That's what the snake says, gliding over the ground
or climbing an oak with the same sleek movement,
nothing attached, her body a clean line.

When the snake loves, she comes together
in a breeding ball, a writhing knot
of snakes wrapped around each other,
in which she cannot imagine she is distinctive,

then slides off to her solitary life. She can even leave
behind her own skin when she tires of it,
stockings strewn in the weeds.

Hold yourself
apart like that, and maybe you can take pleasure
from the something new
this life is always slipping away to.

Be like the rattlers that boy sold to circuses.
He'd store a snake in ice.

Her blood would slow, and she'd stiffen,
but she'd survive his cold.

When the handler pulled the snake from the box
under the bright tent, the spotlight,
and the audience's rapt eyes,
she was ready to soften,

quick to undulate again,
slithering through the warmth
of a man's tough, tattooed hands.

When there were backwoods, when a person was
badly cut and bleeding, it used to be

the bloodstopper would come. She'd focus on the wound,
and chant a Bible verse, a secret charm,

or only the command, *Stop, blood, stop.*
And it would be stopped, by her will. Who today

would call that woman's way of fixing her eyes on another
a perceptive art? We do not have to keep things back now,

but break the tradition of holding in,
the grace of people closing up where they're weak.

We draw them out, the reddest admissions.

Tonight, when the trainload of coal, trailing ash
from the power plant, passed, I had no mournfulness left
for the suffering caused by the energy my lights
spend. Like the film images of the clouds that form
when the mountains are blown apart—how they pulse,
fill the screen, obscure everything—that's how blurred
my mind was by the thought of what I wanted: another
whiskey. New boots. Possessions in numbers. To turn
and go back down the street to where the painter
who is not my husband but looks at me so long
holds his brush suspended above a palette of reds.
So much desire, and to desire goodness is no escape.
I will always end questioning what I've chosen,
regretting some greed. Or regretting that I slept cold
while the bulbs I left on burned into another day
when I would take nothing of what I wanted in my arms,
risk nothing that would bring color to my cheeks.

You claim the clear water in wilderness on the far coast
is better because streams are filtered by mosses and lichens
of forests never logged, and the lakes are filled by snowpack,
white that has only ever touched white, melting to make water.
A fallen leaf can be seen over 100 feet below the surface of a lake—
such precision. An argument for purity. But is that what you want
to argue for, stranger? You're leaning closer. Waters here are murky.
It's an ancient, worn landscape with slow-moving rivers that let
hundreds of kinds of life evolve. Your crystalline creeks house only one
species of fish and are considered complete. More fish than you
could ever count and whole cars lie beneath these bodies of mine.
I swam over a wreck for years without seeing it until I grew old enough,
got long legs, and something soft and slick wrapped around my toe,
a seat belt unloosed, rotten backseat leather unfurling in current,
drawing me down toward the metal below. Imagine where such
waters could let you drift. Though not many would argue rusted cars
were virtues. How about cows that swim the river? Call them cow-brutes,
call them milking-critters, call them beasties, in the vernacular
of this place where things are named twice or oddly to honor complexity.
To make them familiar, because this is worked land, intimate. Or to
make them sound bigger and fiercer, to flatter what we tame.
How do you like to be talked to? The cattle slipping on muddy banks—
yes, they cloud the water, but have you watched the way they drop
their meaty bodies in on hot days, graceless but trusting? That abandon.
You'd have to enter my house like that. You'd have to be unafraid
of stumbling on sagging floors, into low doorframes, features
of old structures, the past, people I know. They've always known me.
And I am regaining my footing in this conversation; there are more species
of salamanders in the Southern Appalachians than in any other
temperate region. Come home with me. Come in and tell me I can have
everything. That all of this I love survives, the farms that strove only for
subsistence, content with the providence of junk piles, pearl and diamond

darters, the rarer fauna, the multiplicity of trees, you, the charm of you
so new each move crackles. Say I don't have to give anything up, I can keep
loving it all, and touch your arm, in this land where science has yet to name
many creatures, as rich in breeds as the tropics, land studded with trailers
and slash heaps that blaze into great fires, of plenty, even excess.

▪ 2 ▪

ANOTHER WORLD

Dams create power by holding back
the forward rush of rivers. In the news,
there are photos out of South America,

old women who won't leave
the land troops have come to claim,
for construction. Their bodies
pause the flood, for a few hours.
See the strange proportions
of power, how strong the will to hold back.

On summer outings I swam over houses
in Carolina. Whole towns lay below
our lakes, but I didn't think of it as home
to the largest engineering project in the world.
Fontana dam had spanned our river
with a wall, a sleek structure, larger, stronger
than the greatest rock faces, which were
creased, had faults, could fall.

The sight of rock crushers biting
into mountains was appealing if you were
angry at someone, a historian wrote.
And soon enough, there was cause to be—
for one dam, thirteen hundred families
evicted, ninety cemeteries dug up.

Shaped like a butterfly,
that's the Tennessee Valley. But it is no
flighted, light thing. My thoughts should swim

with darkness, hearths gone cold, emptied graves,
fish slipping slick-bellied over stones,
when I turn on an electric lamp.

■

Dams all down this valley. Dams planned
for Suriname, Mexico, Panama, Patagonia,
Costa Rica. Already, so many rivers
are dammed that the earth is thrown off.
It's tilting on its axis, the angle
measurably altered.

Or is this not about change? Can I say
nothing ever is over? People now
are not so different than before. I pause
to watch my reflection in water. It warps
with some shift, goes strange, then stands again,
and I am reminded of an arrogant, younger self,
or a relative years gone. Who doesn't live
in the sway of the power of what's pent up
behind them?

■

So the people on the continents
below ours want a stop, to stay
where they speak their rare languages,
in rain forests, among orchids still unnamed.

What Fontana families have been asking for,
for more than fifty years, is to have roads
built to those cemeteries still above water,
the footpaths to which did not show on maps

and were cut off long ago. They want to go back
to their dead.

Let me keep it. Let me get it back.
Aren't our feelings common?
That I'm living on the shore beyond
where I belong, that I just passed
over it in a loud motorboat.

■

Power always is sent to serve regions other
than where it is made. Still, some dam designers,
calling themselves *engineers, enemies of error,*
meant well. What work but building
was there left for locals, with farmland
eroded? Everyone was trying
to hold things in place.

I have done as much. Didn't I
spend hot childhood days damming
up creeks, feeling like a creator,
maybe even a savior, piling debris to slow
water into a little pool to float in a little while?

■

At Fontana, in spring, lines of daffodils
lead into the lake, along where flights
of stairs had been, to the drowned town.

There is much to regret, but let be the love
for what was. I won't follow that path
down. But I would admire the bulbs

of surviving daffodils. Also the blazes
of color on the cheeks of tribes
come to the cities in protest, their timeless
tattoos, what looks like the past
storming the streets.

There was no electric light, but so much sun
in the tropics, and bunches of bananas
strung from the ceiling, yellow chandeliers
by day. By night, bats flew to them,
hollowing out the fruits and tunneling
entirely inside the second skins. Our skins
and bodies shone and were shadowed
flawless in the lanterns' slight, forgiving
light. For years, only smoothed forms
exited beds, unbent from washtubs. How
could today, compared, look? Thinking back
is a burrowing, a blinding, slipping deep
into the past's pulp, scented and pearly.
The sticky wings fold in and still—

No elegy is only for one quarter of the earth.
I've known another where
the single man who spoke my language

was named Mr. Sorrows
and had come to be there by shipwreck.
He explained to me why monkeys inhabit trees

and fish, the sea. How birds got feathers
to rise from water but kept their webbed feet.
Why we live in memory

and, when we leave a place,
wings spread wide, we might think,
our old ways are still folded between our toes,

into our deepest furrows.
He told tales of origin
while his land was held apart from him

by an ocean, an element
no human body was made to enter
and from which we will not ascend.

You don't want the story about the soft clutch
of monkeys' toes, how monkeys swung

languorous from limbs, showering down fruit.
But rather, the one about how

the blue-eyed Abando boy's body hung
after he was lynched for robbing our house,

for robbing any place ever left empty.
You are not as interested in fruit—

hearing how it was heavy and pendulous
through the forest, a forest hung

with bunches of bananas, *zapotes* that fell
erupting orange custard among rambutans—

as in the way thieves ripped jewelry from women's
ears, hooks pulled through the lobes, so they hung

with rubies of blood. You listen more closely
when I tell of how I clung

to the reins when a drunk whipped my horse
into a frenzy and out, swimming, to sea,

than of the tame iguana I hung
in a bird cage, fine wire formed into a palace.

Even though I fed him on hibiscus,
and could describe so many lush, red flowers,

folding from the mouth.

Once Jerónimo Matute rode a horse up
to the bar, ordered a drink, and swallowed the shot
without dismounting. Many evenings,

his horse sauntered in as my mother served dinner
and he shouted, *Mejor al tiempo que invitado!*
Better on time than invited. Most dawns,

he galloped out to sea, plastered sand in his gray
chest hair, stripped the patch from his white,
blinded eye, and shouted of his strength. Today,

he died. But doesn't someone on the continent
where once I knew such color still shade
under an elephant leaf, suck sugarcane, slam

dominoes down on an echoing oil drum?
The game goes on, the rum around the back room,
that life—

where it was Matute's whoops or howler monkeys
that stirred me from my child's sleep. It's the loss
of him, it's sympathy for another. That's why I weep,

waking to only black coffee, all this silent morning.

I was holding a chick in one hand
when I was given my first cup of coffee
in the other. This was deep in the bush,
where coffee was served thick black
with a pot of warm water, to cut it to taste.
I did not want to let the chick go, to free
my hand. So I drank the cup straight,
without adding water, without the sugar
children were allowed. That chick was
broken-legged and tame, it wouldn't
have run away. But I couldn't risk losing
the softness I had grasped. And now I never
consider water, because I have two hands and
got a taste, too, for the burning and strong.

How to cook on fire, carry water,
light with candles, keep bags close
to her side in crowds, use a knife
to clean her nails when hitchhiking
(just so the drivers could see she
had it), and use her teeth to get the fruit
off mango pits—my mother
learned how to do all of this. Also,
how to find a money changer, watch
the men on corners calling, *Colones*,
and choose one with a good rate,
one to trust. The little I may know
as well as her is the hanging feeling
of the moment when she handed a man
her money. The waiting for him to run or
begin passing bills back. The uttering of,
Change me. Into a woman
who can live in this world.

They say the king of the indigenous people's one duty now
is to pretend he does not speak Spanish, that it is possible

to get along with only his own language. *Home Creek*
is how English-speaking West Indian settlers knew the place

we lived. But Spanish-speaking officials wrote *Hone Creek*.
The word *hone* as a mistake—it's not so strange, considering

inaccuracy is what is refined, trying to hold an impression
over time. The name *Home* wasn't saved in any written record.

So there is no way to go back. When I was a baby,
before I could try to speak, native women swam the creek,

covering only their breasts because, they said, they were
born with the other parts (the ones we might

call private). The breasts are an embarrassment
because they change over time. And how I have grown—

But no more articulate. With their first cries, babies
parted from mothers speak better of the need for the known.

And the want to be understood—it has been stated by the silence
of elders, and the willful, the wistful, mapmakers' errors.

They live in the cloud forests. Why would they come down?
Margay. Manigordo. The arboreal cats. With dark markings
around their eyes, applied like liner. Long legs tossed like scarves
around branches. Lounging, they drop their lids. Drippingly,
they lift their limbs. Like juveniles. *Manigordo*—it's not wrong
to give an ocelot a name that translates to *fat paws*. To call
an exotic animal girlish. They are like girls, all their lives
looking as if they're still growing into their feet, with all their
rare certainty, above threat in the trees. With all their
endangered beauty. You do not know it's ending, in that time when
you remain beautiful.

Shouldn't it be that the past is as insignificant
as third world countries appear on maps? But each element
sings. Or it growls or it screams. The buses are loaded

with caged *jaguarundi* beneath blankets and children calling
empanadas, empanadas calientes in the aisles. I too staggered
down those crowded passageways, and through many

vivid places, where bougainvillea and cripples' feet
drug the streets. All moves were marked,
by the border officials who slit fingers to test for fever,

smearing blood on slides at every crossing
over a rusty bridge. From the guard's tower, after a time—
it would be a blessing to look at last from a distance and find

that what has been determines less. But later tries
to make yourself are a lightly perfumed, translucent cream
laid over the inflexible, boned structure of your sunburned face.

Boundaries and statements like, *This is how it is now,* are thin lines
scratched over jungles, immense and evergreen.

On that black sand coast, a woman can say *pink dress*
in English. That is the mark I have made.
When they were to walk too far or do work too hard
for me to bear, my family left me with the neighbor,
her nine children. She'd strip off my clothes, line me up
with the rest, and bathe us by dousing us with buckets.
The clothes she put back on me were not always my own.
I wept, wanting to be distinguishable again. She
memorized the foreign syllables I kept crying to repeat
to my parents, so they could tell the cause of my terrible
suffering. *My pink dress*, was what she sounded out.
How weak, what foolishness. Years, I imagined how she
must have looked down on me. Until I heard she'd left
her family for a white man. She'd had twelve children
by then and never gotten what she wanted. Her explanation
for what she'd done: *I wanted a chance to have a baby*
with blue eyes.

I was four when a column of army ants, twenty thousand
or more, raided the house, washing the floor black.
I climbed on a table, above the biting clamor,
and crouched, legs cramping, wanting water,
watching the ants swarm. Hours, they preyed
on termites thick in the beams and scorpions fell
writhing and covered from the ceiling. Until,
at once, all the ants, indistinguishable,
streamed away to flush birds from the bushes,
or small cats from swamps, and eat their bones bare.
Seeing such exotic sights, such a sweeping gesture
as ants ever traveling, each day invading a new place,
hunting through my home—how did it shape me?
Not into a column, a solid thing. What I marvel at
most now is common, little, individual. To have met him.
And to see him again. So often that I'd know his back
by the slant way he walks, in any crowd. This better
than living among the numerous and always ranging hungry.

After the thief, dark-skinned, blue-eyed
Abando, died, the break-ins continued.

His sweetheart remembered him, his
ways, and this is about love. She burned

off padlocks, filling them with gasoline,
setting them alight, so they burst open—

a story I tell you because I want
your attention. For you to come for dinner again.

To stay as I lay silver in expected places
around the table. To keep listening until

you think of one chair here as your own.
Then I'll admit a softer truth: All she stole

was a jar of honey and—I can see, she wanted
to keep something close—my locket

to hang around her neck.

The legends of that locale are called bellyful tales because
they are told when no one is hungry. The only task then
is talk, for tongues to vary, abundantly, the few themes.

And aren't we allowed indulgences? Having lived once,
then the leisure to tell it over, having loved one,
the chance to lose ourselves again—

The dish of the region is rundown, a pot of coconut milk,
plantains, peppers, octopus, squid, any scraps, always cooking
on woodstoves—a broth of what could have been waste.

No, there's nothing new in it. But it couldn't be richer.
What would you rather have than a thing you know
spiced and simmered, spoken and seconded,

in another's accent?

1.

When plantains ripened, when there was gold
to gather from above, tribal people joined
cane to make rafts. A whole family,
their whole harvest, rode the river to town.

At the end of a trip, they let their vessel
wash on. They tied, trusted, then left
the twine and cuttings. There was nothing
they had to carry back on the walk upstream.

What motion might such boatmen have made
when the last plantain was unloaded?
Just an opening of the palm
that held the rope, or a shoving away?

May the practice of the pose of release
ease their loss now. Dams are stopping
their river and their language is drying
in the mouths of the last speakers.

Can I hope that when they let go
it was with a gesture toward endlessness?
May I suggest that they built with abundant
materials and can build again?

2.

I can't claim to understand the end
of a culture just because there is a house I loved
I no longer live in. The particulars I miss are so
slight (and so, I have felt, irreplaceable).

But, I know that any travel away
from where one has been, however small,
scrapes a kind of bottom. Trying to ease passage—
that's why Americans dynamite our own rivers.

Tourists boat where I live now, floating on the cushions
of rafts, heavy with gear and worry. So I can't address
larger sufferings. How about, then, compassion,
for them, for what seems foreign in my own country?

I'll say it's touching—the tourists—how they work
at saving their own way of life, with first-aid kits,
food on ice, folding chairs. When I moved, I too
wanted to keep everything dear with me.

We don't know what to do for others. But care
is what loads overlarge packs. We fasten
life jackets on dogs. Even in slight rapids,
we hold the body in reach, the one child, tight.

■ 3 ■

ANOTHER TELLING

Smile like a crescent moon, a hook
that can haul a man in.

    Be a shadow
    dragging from the hand you hold.

    ■

Wait at your one window, loyal
with your lamp.

    Say there is nothing unspoiled—others' shine,
    distant cities, dampen every horizon's hem.

    ■

Gather close into what bright circle
a candle gives.

    Let any wind be a snuffing blow.

    ■

If unaccustomed to arising at night
in houses with no electricity, still feel, expectant,
along walls for light switches.

    Or, even when there is
    a switch to reach for, must you move through
        houses that could be lit, leaving them dark?

THE TREATMENT WAS FROGS, OR,
THE TRADITION WAS HONEY

There are many old treatments for each trouble.
It could be the butter was witched, cursed

by an ill-wisher so the cream would not gather.
A woman might have stabbed knives or pokers,

hot from the fire, into cream to drive out evil,
and believed the touch of the tools she used

would show on the skin of the witch,
welts and gashes marking him. That's one tradition

you could keep alive; you could look for such signs
in the faces you see. But a woman could also

charm quarrelsome cream by dropping something
silver into the churn. The idea of a locket

enveloped in white, a gleaming sliver
sliding into a rich bath, might be what you carry on.

Then butter will thicken in its mold—whatever you make
your custom—as if it had always been set firm.

History was once written to instruct or
persuade. The church has taught us well.
This is how to be a good king. And an *ars historica*
is what two friends speak, over wine. So let us
describe this evening in a constructive style.
The man was happy with how the woman
listened and the closeness between them was
enough. Now you can take from this a lesson
on how to be a good woman. Love one man
wholly and learn not to grieve over what you can
never give others. We will leave the friend
unnamed. After all, who wants sources? No one
liked the first cited history, unoriginal, uninterpreted,
and lacking in purpose to color the facts. It was gray
outside, cold, and the friend went away. She stayed,
facing the café window a while. Here's how
to see it: All the people out there, heads bowed
into the winter, did not look at what they passed
because they had already determined the conclusion
at which they wanted to arrive. The way it should
appear, as it is depicted, is that all of us now
are heading toward something better. Is that not
how history would have it? We will illustrate
the walkers' forward strides. We will excise
the way the woman glances at a new face,
then grooms her hair, that gesture of pausing
and pushing back.

We give artifacts galleries, glass, locks,
handle them wearing white cotton gloves,
to protect them from change. Though already
they are corroded, discolored, cracked,
we believe our time can be stilled.

So we are at our best, making a great wish,
reassuring relics: The blows you withstood
were before our time. The damage
to be done, done in the past.

Only in museums do we now display
such hushed devotion, browsing crowds'
heads bowed toward the revered.

The historical man deserves our hearts;
his way of behaving has been determined.
(In the Woodland Period, we know
there was art, ceremony, cultivation.)
He will not disappoint. And us?

From the shape of an arrow, we learn
what was hunted. From the ax of exotic copper,
with whom there was trade. If conservators
are someday to consider the shards of our pots,
may they find, more than fractures, caresses
patterning our bodies of clay.

Archives collect old photos, evidence of endurance—women's faces
stretched long as laundry hung out to dry but caught in the rain,

men with copperheads slung over their shoulders, hatchets in hand,
fields of tobacco filling every middle distance, acres of work always

between the subject and the shelter or church on the horizon. And now,
we seem to have agreed hardship is what's historical. What's assured

to be everlasting. Of all I see, what we'd likely say looks timeless
is the black and white view of cattle with snow along their spines,

scraping at drifts with hooves, working to uncover grass. Generations
have been seeing that same hungry scene. But can't we change the constants,

choose different images? Aren't there also beauty bush's berries vibrant purple
just under the ice? Haven't there always been? In those dusty folders,

there are photos of a wood-carver displaying shelves of shining toys he's made,
giraffes as a man who has never left the county imagines such creatures.

And a gladiola farm, a family standing in the field won from mountains,
kept clear of rocks, arms full of glads. On some negatives,

the photographer has penciled directions: *Take off that shadow.*

I was the kind to note the apple trees heaviest
with blooms now were the ones

with trunks broken by snow in winter.
The kind drawn to the company

of antique circular sawmills in outbuildings,
liable to study dents hammered into the blades,

seeing that when they spun fast enough,
the warped metal flattened out and the tension

added to its strength. You understand the appeal—
the lessons about rewards to come. But what of

the mornings when I woke and rain had turned
furrows on the mountain that had always borne

the shape of water into springs again,
with daylilies opening along them. Help me

to give thanks as well as the porches of my home place,
every ceiling painted light blue. All the colors—

and the builders of these houses made a likeness
of the sky, looked no further.

Rain is lines, barely, I squint to see.
It's a quality, evenly over the whole
outward view. It's what moves the leaves
when I cannot say why else they would bow.
How could one draw, how can I word, this?

"The Greeks too are calm; a man hurling
a discus will be shown in the moment
in which he gathers his strength,"
the painter said. It is the pause before motion
that he understands he can try to capture.
So might my words, still all this time, have been
hunched before a leap, hunkered beneath
a shelter—an old roof, a rock, rain
running off the lip.

Though it falls, rain is a constant. No point of origin
or end, no definite edges to any drop. Even
as it happens, rain's time is the before. Because
it pauses people. "I will not go out in it, yet," we say.
At the window, I am preparing, my boots and coat,
to state something sure, or sufficient.

Then rain becomes, after months of it,
only a condition in which to carry on.
Rain is the first sound I hear when I wake,
the first feeling on my skin when I step out.
I continue. What could be more affirmative
than deciding "never mind" and beginning
a walk though clouds convene overhead?

But if I say I sense, foremost in the world,
winter rain, it may not seem praise.
You see me as somber. How else could I be?
Heavy is the dress for this weather.

Let the picture be judged not by the likeness
it makes. See how my lines stray—
toward sentiment. I use the broad, over-wet brush
of the rain. The trees, as done by it, are no certain
species, neither needled nor bare, not even
branched or broken into any parts.
They're blurs, they're great blots.
By great, I mean not just spreading,
but grand.

I mean gray. If I chose for the image a palette
that reflects, not reality, but bent, I would
celebrate in gray. Winter's brambles and rosehips
are red in only a few bright daubs, too distinct,
too select. Would contentment not be the color
of the soaked ground, what stretches on, sodden?

I take as the figure for my acclaim
even the disfavored rain.

To see a landscape, a viewer
assembles parts, adds trees to the rocks,
reconciles their battle with roots,
turns the boundaries of fences
into the blanket stitch of the one
piece. Is this not like love, how I was
pulled through years by little intimacies,
focusing on the soft skin behind his ear,
the shady spots familiar oaks form
at one time of day?

■

Let me draw these connections.
Also, lines between myself and
those who came before. I must
believe adages, that the new builds off
the worn. And that this mountain
landscape I come from speaks of
ancestors who, in settling such terrain,
showed a tendency to carry on.

■

For cultures to show progress, empires
must expand outward across the land.
As after long loving, who we once were
becomes obscured, pebbles
in the grass. Painters tend
to pebbles for a time,
but there is a whole panorama to make.

■

Older. Yet I can't grow old enough
to stop seeing love in every line, like
painters who continue painting
landscape. The less our lives have to do
with land, the more we need
to look at it in frames.

■

And as the land that was a field
grows towers, blooms streetlights,
all the more I remember
how he was the first day
he stepped toward me,
holding bottles of wine
that would unloose our sweet
words, while all of the words
of another kind
were still beyond the horizon.

■

In the past, people built cabins
in coves between mountains,
off to the south side, as if to show
the eye into the scene, their
low doorways gentle welcomes
to summits beyond.
But this time's assuming structures
clutter the center of the canvas,
step in front of mountains.
What can I add now? Early efforts,
in weathered wood, look romantic.

Later tries at making a life, rattling
aluminum buildings.

■

A few branches brush the foreground,
saplings lean in from the edges,
and a wide space opens beyond:
a classic composition. The view
of a small animal peeking out
from safety is the way we paint the world.
And I liked how things looked
from such shelter, didn't want to watch as
a hunter, sighting down the shaft of an arrow,
about to bound forward. I wanted to stay
nestled in the leaves.

■

As Europeans claimed wilderness,
conquered territory, painters
cleared trees from their minds
to create vantage points and placed
landmarks in better settings.
To love what you have—a good
aspiration. But inconstancy
is sometimes required. So, I too must
move mountains. I must come to know
destruction, how to be driven by want
toward another.

■

The line of beauty, art theorists
say, is the one that bends

from where we expected.
Because it is not fixed, because
it does not stay, it attracts the eye,
and is alive.

■

How good then,
today, to find myself staring
at the tendons in a man's neck,
between them, his breath. I could follow
them a long way, down beneath
his collar. First, I should speak, see how
his chest shifts through the shirt,
just in the act of turning to me.

■

Next, we could talk of buffalo trails
through mountains that settlers walked
that became our well-traveled roads.
And of the painter's knife, how it cuts some,
moving across the thick pigments
already laid, but carries
the brightest green.

Velvet: It's a verb where I am visiting.
I speak to myself the word for

what elk horns do in spring, how
they get a soft covering, for comfort

in a new place, Western peaks
striking out toward the sky.

Antlers grow
an inch a day here. Could I

become a part of another region?
Yes, antlers expand

following the pattern of the father—
the young's prongs and spaces

positioned the same as those before.
But elk's grounds

are gone. Relocated, they've learned
to survive a landscape of stone

where only seven species of tree
make spare shadows on the snow.

Could I begin to see the beauty
of austerity? I could

set a life on this coast, in
the country of recent history

where the oldest cemeteries
are younger than most houses I've known.

I could not talk of cemeteries,
not collect

the fallen horns of past seasons.
Aren't there actions other

than looking for what I can hold on to?
Abandon: That can

be an adjective—and admirable.
Like a herd toward the horizon, I can

run with it. With it, I say. And so
not alone at all.

A blond body, the darker streak down the back—
a cougar takes shape in the road ahead.
I am walking alone, at dusk, hours to anywhere, the spell
of my truck's workings broken down.
But in a way, there is still a magic.

The cougar lifts its head and shifts
into a deer.

Then out of the miles of nothing on a back route
and the worse possibilities
of what another person finding me here
could do, forms a silver car
driven by a kind young man.

Western deer have dark markings, black tails.
They're not like the Southern whitetails
I grew up among, those bodies
made just for flashing signals of alarm.

Now, it is different. Now, things have changed.
I say those charmed phrases.

I won't dream women do not have to first learn
what violences exist especially for them
to feel such gratitude while walking,
only blistered feet abused, by themselves.

I won't wish that the characters vanished
into the woods aren't the soonest turned to legend,
that lives don't have to be lost, or nearly,
for us to discern the fine solidity of their substance.

I turn the event (with a sparkle, or a cloud
of dust from the gravel) into
one for which I am thankful.
In the real wonder that is the human
moral-making way, forever
finding occasion to be glad.

The predator's eyes go gentle as a doe's
because they are a doe's. The man rides up, in shining
rims and mirror tinted windows.
And the sunset, which we love for its colored summary,
gloriously reimagines the day.

At least once, I will praise high-rises.
Such structures may fall, with our way
of living. My details may be quickly outdated.
But I want to admire the silhouettes of guests
in the windows of tall hotels, one-night homes,
when they step to the glass to look out, that impulse
everyone has that undoes apartness. And cell phones,
how people walking toward me holding them
on their shoulders appear, at first, to cock their heads
in interest. They are attentive—to someone
chosen above all around them that can stumble or crash,
a voice fuller than flesh. Also the fortune
of pulling into a parking lot just as dance class
is letting out, the sequined seconds,
before they are closed into alike cars and sped away,
when little girls fill all the spaces. I shine, I glow
from the frivolous gesture of a stranger who takes my coat
when I enter a building. Of course, I could do it myself.
But he takes my coat in tribute to the change
from outside to in and passing time—our half hour
in the same heated comfort. The bright fabric,
a briefly fashionable shade, he hangs, a banner
for our lucky, needless lives.

Gutting the deer, down among the blasts
of fallen leaves, golden and red against
the gray of winter pending, and the red,
of course, of blood, and the more various
shades of insides—the yellows and purples
and pure, resistant whites you don't think of
until you're doing the work—is not what
strummed, beat in, certainly not what
set to singing, my senses.

It was earlier, before the hunter made his shot,
lying in the cabin alone, listening to samba—
Brazil, bronzed skin, and costumes tailored
to display it dancing out of headphones
powered by battery, from an improbable gift
mailed by a friend. While I wore flannel,
thick, stiffening with blood, and held
the basic makings of a life in my hands
(this organ is for breathing in, that for emitting
waste) it was with wishfulness for what could be
that I was occupied. It was thinking
far beyond here, of the future, a tune
from the genre of expectant compositions,
with which I hummed.

And I remembered the sender, her profuse dresses:
Always satin for ballroom dancing, white, of course,
for her wedding, and then full swirls draping
the stomach that keeps giving her children. She intends
to have eight. I am too timid to dance and even without
electricity or a phone, hours from any neighbor,
in all that loneliness, I could not imagine how I could

afford to keep just one. But deer ticks
don't let go of their host body even when it's dead,
I was reminded, down running the knife through
the infested fur of the belly. And I held on
to some idea of elegance, or rather a smaller hope,
not for a dramatic partner dance, but that some things
can slip into a matched step, one person caring
for or feeding from another.

Walking home with the deer's head
held by one antler in my hand (it was too bloody
to put in the truck) I talked to it. He probably couldn't hear
or didn't want my explanations. And though I did not
tell him how poor I was or promise to eat only berries
henceforth, when I arrived at the house, his eyes,
which had been flung open all afternoon as I did
what I must to his muscles, had eased closed.

I did wish I could feed on berries. Blackberries
were the closest thing to the company of other
women in those woods, with the sensitive flesh
that tripled warmth when days offered it, had sweetness
washed away by a hard rain, and dried out if left long.
So I was too remote to have friends and one cannot live by
plucking softly food from bushes that go on undamaged—
still there is a shine of a rhinestone kind inside. In the guts
of deer, or any animal, unwrapped from the layers
of membrane, there is luminousness—wet coils, taut sacks,
organs with oil-slick opal sheen. Inside my friend,
a pink furl, another satisfied desire, floats and grows,
fills her hollows. She's expecting again.

And I have my expectations. As did the buck who intended
to continue, certainly on to the next episode of grass
between ferns, maybe over the hill to the apples, or farther—

beliefs that could have made him happy. I, planning
my winter of eating, my store of meat, assumed
I'd go on living. That day, there within the boundaries
of my small property, whether or not I'd noticed, while crowds
clapped on to other rhythms in warmer countries, a wish
of mine (mine and not everyone's, not his) was granted.
All aspirations are wild, maybe greedy, maybe made great
by sequins or spleen.

The night the bull broke loose,
there was much to learn. Like,
when a bull lowers his head to charge,
step close. This is when you can
slip a rope around his neck. Or,
when the men, butted and bruised
with rope-burned hands, give up,
make a path of sweet feed.
The bull will follow it inside the fence,
and, quietly, you can close the gate.
But let's not look to make allegories,
for any meaning beyond the marvel
of a bull, tangled in a broken rope,
sheltering in a culvert, stamping, snorting—
the singular sound that echoed in that metal.
You have a life in which such stories
are not symbols. You too held on
to the rope when the bull ran. You
sometimes flew, sometimes followed
on your knees down the mountain, noting
even in brambles, as you bled, the stars.

Deer are always in the picture,
in the wood's clearing where I live,
whether they are stilled in the grass
or running toward the edge,
whether I am remarking,
There they are or *There they go.*

Museum plates disclose,
about the pieces they accompany,
oil, ink, silk screen, silver.
They also demonstrate
that knowing the materials
does not explain an image's effect.

A bear appears in my orchard,
drawn into the open, in midday,
by apples. These are the parts:
fur, flesh, sweetness, surprise. So,
what do I form with them?
I owe this life a tribute.

But I fall short. I admit I am sad
to see the landscape's rare bright space
as no longer safe. I take
his lumbering shape
as a darkness smudged across
the frame that was for light.

My art make more of the world? I wish
I was capable of even imitating one black fiber
caught on the bark of all I've been shown—
And if I have skill enough only for laments?

See that this is at least an effort
I was moved to, and however I use it,
beauty the material.

When the river flooded, when
I was a child, I boated
around the fields. And so it began,
my myth-making. I recall that altered time
foremost. I float.

Transformative washes
over the world—the time of evening when
I can have a drink, being in love,
the lyric way of speaking—that's what
I've turned out to live for.

Though I know what's more worthy
is the solid ground
and those who stood
on and worked it. My mother
would have been chopping
food she'd grown in those fields
while I was drifting over them.

I was heading out beyond
the sounds unintentionally but always
made by cooking—
not a special bell, no lifting song,
the economical and earthly summons.

There must have been, as every night,
the clunk of cast iron and a heavy meal
I was little help in preparing.

But what struck me
was the rarity: watching a lost garden.

The leaves wafted, the rounds
of fruits that had hung,
though ruined, were buoyant now.
Broken by refraction, they changed
to baubles I wanted.

The flood was a costumer, a jeweler.
And the way water cut ordinary sights,
that was appealing labor:
making stone toss about weightless light.

If there was a score to those years,
it was the somber percussion

of feed in a bucket, how we would
shake grain to call the cows, chickens,

kibble to call the dogs, call voicelessly
whatever would come. We spoke softly.

We knew shouting and chasing
what you want doesn't work. We always

had something to say
and never needed to talk about ourselves.

Look, she's hungry. She wants more.
Watch the funny way she does that.

Don't you love it? I didn't want dogs,
but there the strays were, in the ditches,

on the doormat. I let them in.
And so a life makes itself, awhile.

She wants to be kept forever.
I thought I would live in such a way,

walking about my small chores
in the stretching evening, forever.

It is not only strays who are disappointed.
A person may be kind and still possess

the command that means she will be
the one who decides to leave.

Even if it feels like all she has
is what finds her by chance, lingers by choice,

her companionship a woods' cove
some happen into. The score to that time,

a common contentment that came with no tags
and went unnamed, was the hushed beat

of dogs' feet on dirt, walking with us.
I used them, then, as symbols of how well

I could care for another, though they were becoming
the images of all I would give up,

what I would cry out about missing.
As if those lives had wandered away from me

and I was the one who would run for days
on a scent-memory toward

an end to which I thought I was bound. But toward—
that isn't truly the movement that plays

over in my mind. When the dogs were
happiest, they did not need to be touched,

and no more affection than had been given.
Those were the days when I succeeded

in making love certain. They'd step ahead,
or sit at an angle, however slightly, away.

NOTES

Thanks to those of you who encouraged the writing of this book: Laura, Elisabeth, Rebecca, Rachel, Dave, Collin, Olivia, Deb, all my friends from Warren Wilson, the Gardiner family, and, of course and always, my family.

I am indebted to W. J. T Mitchell's *Landscape and Power* for ideas in the poem "Landscape."

"Wet Not with Weeping" quotes Matisse.

JOHN ASHBERY
Selected Poems
Self-Portrait in a Convex
  Mirror

TED BERRIGAN
The Sonnets

LAUREN BERRY
The Lifting Dress

JOE BONOMO
Installations

PHILIP BOOTH
Selves

JULIANNE BUCHSBAUM
The Apothecary's Heir

JIM CARROLL
Fear of Dreaming:
  The Selected Poems
Living at the Movies
Void of Course

ALISON HAWTHORNE
DEMING
Genius Loci
Rope

CARL DENNIS
Another Reason
Callings
New and Selected Poems
  1974–2004
Practical Gods
Ranking the Wishes
Unknown Friends

DIANE DI PRIMA
Loba

STUART DISCHELL
Backwards Days
Dig Safe

STEPHEN DOBYNS
Velocities: New and Selected
  Poems, 1966–1992

EDWARD DORN
Way More West: New and
  Selected Poems

ROGER FANNING
The Middle Ages

ADAM FOULDS
The Broken Word

CARRIE FOUNTAIN
Burn Lake

AMY GERSTLER
Crown of Weeds: Poems
Dearest Creature
Ghost Girl
Medicine
Nerve Storm

EUGENE GLORIA
Drivers at the Short-Time
  Motel
Hoodlum Birds
My Favorite Warlord

DEBORA GREGER
By Herself
Desert Fathers, Uranium
  Daughters
God
Men, Women, and Ghosts
Western Art

TERRANCE HAYES
Hip Logic
Lighthead
Wind in a Box

NATHAN HOKS
The Narrow Circle

ROBERT HUNTER
Sentinel and Other Poems

MARY KARR
Viper Rum

WILLIAM KECKLER
Sanskrit of the Body

JACK KEROUAC
Book of Sketches
Book of Blues
Book of Haikus

JOANNA KLINK
Circadian
Raptus

JOANNE KYGER
As Ever: Selected Poems

ANN LAUTERBACH
Hum
If in Time: Selected Poems,
  1975–2000
On a Stair
Or to Begin Again
Under the Sign

CORINNE LEE
PYX

PHILLIS LEVIN
May Day
Mercury

PATRICIA LOCKWOOD
Motherland Fatherland
  Homelandsexuals

WILLIAM LOGAN
Macbeth in Venice
Madame X
Strange Flesh
The Whispering Gallery

ADRIAN MATEJKA
The Big Smoke
Mixology

MICHAEL MCCLURE
Huge Dreams: San Francisco
  and Beat Poems

ROSE MCLARNEY
Its Day Being Gone

DAVID MELTZER
David's Copy: The Selected
  Poems of David Meltzer

ROBERT MORGAN
Terroir

CAROL MUSKE-DUKES
An Octave Above Thunder
Red Trousseau
Twin Cities

ALICE NOTLEY
Culture of One
The Descent of Alette
Disobedience
In the Pines
Mysteries of Small Houses

WILLIE PERDOMO
The Essential Hits of Shorty
  Bon Bon

LAWRENCE RAAB
The History of Forgetting
Visible Signs: New and
  Selected Poems

BARBARA RAS
The Last Skin
One Hidden Stuff

MICHAEL ROBBINS
Alien vs. Predator

PATTIANN ROGERS
Generations
Holy Heathen Rhapsody
Wayfare

WILLIAM STOBB
Absentia
Nervous Systems

TRYFON TOLIDES
An Almost Pure Empty Walking

ANNE WALDMAN
Gossamurmur
Kill or Cure
Manatee/Humanity
Structure of the World
  Compared to a Bubble

JAMES WELCH
Riding the Earthboy 40

PHILIP WHALEN
Overtime: Selected Poems

ROBERT WRIGLEY
Anatomy of Melancholy and
  Other Poems
Beautiful Country
Earthly Meditations: New and
  Selected Poems
Lives of the Animals
Reign of Snakes

MARK YAKICH
The Importance of Peeling
  Potatoes in Ukraine
Unrelated Individuals Forming
  a Group Waiting to Cross

JOHN YAU
Borrowed Love Poems
Paradiso Diaspora